Our California

Voyageur Press

Edited by Kari Cornell
Designed by JoDee Mittlestadt
Printed in Hong Kong

03   04   05   06   07   5   4   3   2   1

Library of Congress Cataloging-in-Publication Data

Our California / Kari Cornell, Editor.
   p. cm.
   ISBN 0-89658-031-8
   1. California—Pictorial works. 2. California—Descrip-
tion and travel. 3. California—History, Local—Pictorial
works. I. Cornell, Kari A.
   F862.O97 2003
   917.9404'54—dc21

                        2003007192

Distributed in Canada by Raincoast Books, 9050
Shaughnessy Street, Vancouver, B.C. V6P 6E5

Published by Voyageur Press, Inc.
123 North Second Street, P.O. Box 338, Stillwater, MN
55082 U.S.A.
651-430-2210, fax 651-430-2211
books@voyageurpress.com
www.voyageurpress.com

*Educators, fundraisers, premium and gift buyers, publi-
cists, and marketing managers:* Looking for creative
products and new sales ideas? Voyageur Press books are
available at special discounts when purchased in quanti-
ties, and special editions can be created to your specifica-
tions. For details contact the marketing department at
800-888-9653.

Page 1: *Climbing roses adorn this stone wall in the Carmel Mission Basilica courtyard. (Photograph © Mary Liz Austin)*

Page 2: *The view to the top of the Oregon Tree, one of the giant sequoias that make up General Grant Grove in King's Canyon National Park, is awe inspiring. The grove's trees are believed to be about 3,000 years old. (Photograph © Terry Donnelly)*

Page 3: *Poppies, California goldfields, and cream cups brighten the rolling hills of Antelope Valley California Poppy State Park in Los Angeles County. (Photograph © Larry Ulrich/ Larry Ulrich Stock Photography)*

Page 4: *The Customs House in Monterey, now home to a historical museum and part of Monterey State Historical Park, is the oldest public building in California. (Photograph © Larry Ulrich/Larry Ulrich Stock Photography)*

Page 5, top: *Early morning fog rolls over the Berkley Hills in Alameda County. (Photograph © Gary Crabbe/ Enlightened Images)*

Page 5, bottom: *The V. Sattui Winery tasting room and gourmet cheese shop is cast in the warm light of daybreak. V. Sattui was established in St. Helena, Napa Valley, in the mid 1970s. (Photograph © Chuck Place/Place Stock Photo)*

Page 6: *McWay Creek spills over a rugged cliff to the beach below at Julia Pfeiffer Burns State Park on the Big Sur coast. (Photograph © Mary Liz Austin)*

Page 7: *Surfers talk beneath Oceanside Pier, the longest wooden pier on the West Coast. (Photograph © Gary Crabbe/Enlightened Images)*

Page 9: *A Christmas tree, donated by Snowy Peak Christmas Tree Farm in Forest Hill, brightens the state capitol grounds in Sacramento during the holiday season. (Photograph © Carolyn Fox/Image West Photography)*

Facing page: *Bracken and sword ferns edge this path through Lady Bird Johnson Grove in Redwood National Park. (Photograph © Larry Ulrich/ Larry Ulrich Stock Photography)*

Top: *Oxalis thrives in the lush, moist conditions of Humboldt Redwoods State Park, providing a carpet of green beneath the towering trees. (Photograph © Jim Steinberg)*

Bottom: *Redwoods preserved in Jedediah Smith Redwoods State Park are believed to be about 2,000 years old. Redwoods can grow as tall as 367 feet and reach 22 feet in diameter. (Photograph © Frank S. Balthis)*

The rocks and surf at Wilson Rock, located near Crescent City in Redwood National Park, are bathed in calm. (Photograph © Willard Clay)

Sunlight filters through the mist in this northern coastal forest. (Photograph © Jim Steinberg)

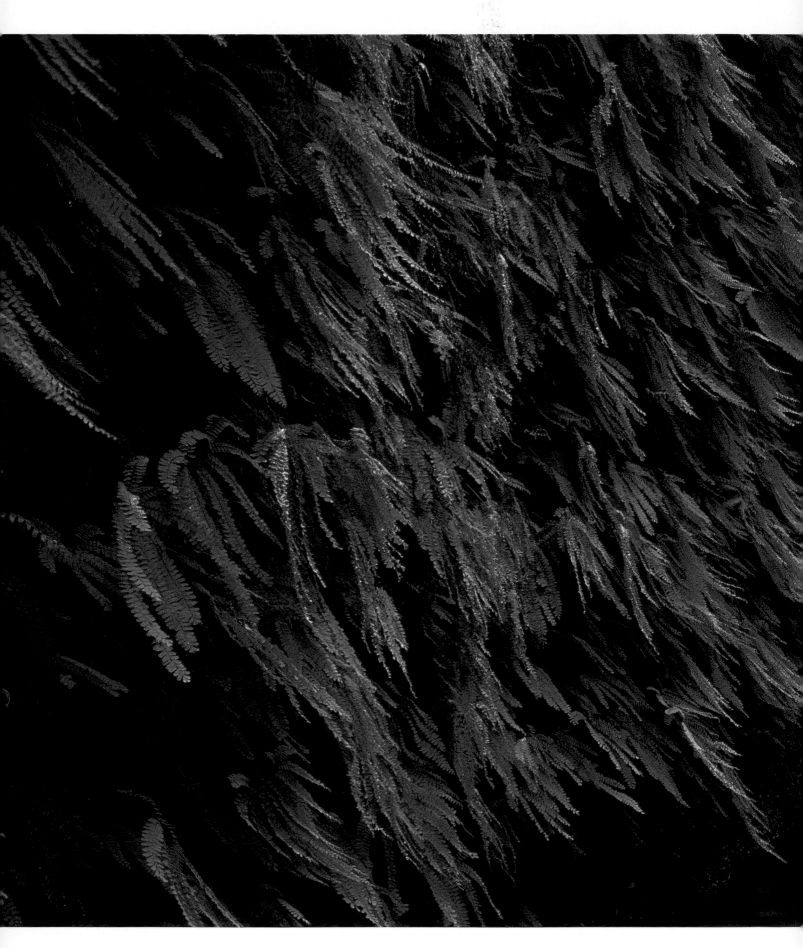

Five-finger ferns climb a moss-covered wall in Fern Canyon, Prairie Creek Redwoods State Park. (Photograph © Chuck Place/ Place Stock Photo)

Facing page: *The beaches along the Redwood National Park coast are adorned with driftwood. (Photograph © Gary Alan Nelson)*

Left: *Roosevelt elk make their home in Prairie Creek Redwoods State Park, part of Redwoods National Park. (Photograph © Susan Cole Kelly)*

Above: *Fire damage is evident on the trunk of this redwood in Lady Bird Johnson Grove. Redwood bark retains moisture, making the trees somewhat resistant to fire. (Photograph © Jim Steinberg)*

Facing page: *Lupine and yarrow frame a view of the Pacific Ocean from High Bluff along Coastal Drive in Redwood National Park. (Photograph © George Wuerthner)*

Above: *Burney Falls in Shasta National Forest drops 129 feet over a verdant moss- and fern-covered cliff. (Photograph © Gary Crabbe/Enlightened Images)*

Mount Shasta's snowy peak rises 14,162 feet, making it the second-tallest mountain in the Cascade Range (Mt. Rainer in Washington State is first). (Photograph © George Wuerthner)

The sun rises with the mist over Grass Lake and Mount Shasta. (Photograph © Larry Ulrich/Larry Ulrich Stock Photography)

Right: *A skier tests his skill on the slopes near Lake Tahoe. (Photograph © Larry Prosor)*

Below: *Lake Tahoe assumes a peaceful tranquility in the warm light of a winter sunrise. (Photograph © Willard Clay)*

Lassen Peak (10,457 feet), formed during a series of eruptions between 1914 and 1917, is one of the last active volcanoes in the Continental United States. In 1916, the federal government set aside the surrounding land to create Lassen Volcanic National Park. (Photograph © George Wuerthner)

Above: *When designing the Ahwahnee Hotel, Gilbert Stanley Underwood used granite boulders and native timbers to make the building blend with its surroundings. (Photograph © Susan Cole Kelly)*

Facing page: *This view of Upper Yosemite Falls has become synonymous with Yosemite National Park. The upper and lower falls together measure 2,425 feet, making them the highest waterfall in North America. (Photograph © Gary Crabbe/Enlightened Images)*

Above: *Half Dome casts an orange-hued reflection in the Merced River. The Yosemite landmark rises one mile above the valley floor, with a summit of 8,840 feet. (Photograph © Dennis Flaherty)*

Facing page: *A misty-topped El Capitán looks grand from the valley 4,500 feet below. The peak's great expanse of exposed rock draws rock climbers from around the world. (Photograph © Dennis Flaherty)*

The Tuolumne River winds through Tuolumne Meadows, catching the reflection of the surrounding peaks. (Photograph © Dennis Flaherty)

Mule deer graze in the thick meadows of Yosemite Valley. The park is also home to mountain lions, bobcats, and coyotes. (Photograph © Dennis Flaherty)

Black oak trees diffuse rays of sunlight in El Capitán Meadow. (Photograph © Dennis Flaherty)

Calcified tufa formations define the shoreline of Mono Lake. This brackish body of water covers sixty square miles and is believed to be the oldest lake in North America. (Photograph © Chuck Place/Place Stock Photo)

A kayaker glides through the placid waters of Mono Lake. (Photograph © Larry Prosor)

In 1880, the town of Bodie was a bustling gold mining town of 8,000. (Photograph © Larry Ulrich/Larry Ulrich Stock Photography)

Bodie State Historic Park, home to the biggest ghost town in California, opened in 1962. (Photograph © Dennis Flaherty)

Top: *Time seems to stand still in Downieville, a small town on the northern edge of Gold Country. (Photograph © Larry Angier/Image West Photography)*

Bottom: *This tamarisk tree appears to be the best place to hang your shoes (or anything else) in sunny California. (Photograph © Larry Angier/Image West Photography)*

Christmas lights add a festive air to the old brick buildings in downtown Jackson, once a gold mining settlement. (Photograph © Carolyn Fox/Image West Photography)

Right: *Mark Twain wrote "The Celebrated Jumping Frog of Calaveras County" in honor of frogs like this one and the many others that compete each year in the jumping contest held at the county fair in Angels Camp. (Photograph © Larry Angier/Image West Photography)*

Below: *A clothesline strung across the main street in Angels Camp announces the Frog Jumping Jubilee, which draws thousands of people to the Gold Country town each May. (Photograph © Carolyn Fox/Image West Photography)*

Fairgoers swing in high style at the Dixon May Fair in Dixon, California. (Photograph © Carolyn Fox/Image West Photography)

Above: *These houses, which date from 1913, 1915, and 1919 respectively, line a street in an old Sacramento neighborhood. (Photograph © Chuck Place/Place Stock Photo)*

Facing page: *Country churches like this one in Yolo County are a familiar sight on California backroads. (Photograph © Carolyn Fox/Image West Photography)*

Right: *Sailboats bob in the morning sun on Tomales Bay, Marin County. (Photograph © Gary Crabbe/Enlightened Images)*

Below: *Once a fishing village, Sausalito is now home to a houseboat community and hillside Victorian cottages. (Photograph © Gary Crabbe/ Enlightened Images)*

Horseback riders enjoy a stroll along a Bodega Bay beach in Sonoma County. (Photograph © Gary Crabbe/Enlightened Images)

Above: *Evening sun warms this inviting balcony at the Little River Inn on the Mendocino County coast. (Photograph © Gary Crabbe/Enlightened Images)*

Facing page: *A weathered fence frames the sea stacks in Greenwood Cove, Mendocino County. (Photograph © Mary Liz Austin)*

Facing page: *The original tasting cellar at the Boeger Winery in the Sierra foothills dates from 1872. (Photograph © Carolyn Fox/Image West Photography)*

Left: *Napa Valley grapes ripen on the vine. (Photograph © Gary Crabbe/ Enlightened Images)*

Below: *A new day dawns over the vineyards near Asti in Sonoma County. (Photograph © Gary Crabbe/ Enlightened Images)*

Left: *Flowering mustard grows with vigor in an old Sonoma County vineyard. (Photograph © Carolyn Fox/Image West Photography)*

Top: *Wine barrels await the next grape harvest at the Montevina Winery in Amador County. (Photograph © Larry Angier/Image West Photography)*

Bottom: *A vintner surveys his vineyard during an early morning stroll. (Photograph © Larry Angier/Image West Photography)*

Facing page: *A San Francisco commuter catches the California Street cable car on Nob Hill. (Photograph © Kerrick James)*

Above: *A row of Queen Anne Victorians, known as the "Six Sisters," line up along the eastern side of Alamo Square. With the San Francisco skyline as a backdrop, these houses are one of the most photographed sites in the city. (Photograph © Larry Ulrich/Larry Ulrich Stock Photography)*

City lights sparkle from behind the famous Golden Gate Bridge. (Photograph © Gary Crabbe/Enlightened Images)

Top: *As the sun rises each morning, the Marin County ferry passes Alcatraz Island on its way into downtown San Francisco. (Photograph © Kerrick James)*

Bottom: *The Golden Gate towers reach a height of 746 feet and the bridge spans 3,950 feet across the bay. The bridge, built in the Art Deco style, was completed in 1937. (Photograph © Larry Ulrich/Larry Ulrich Stock Photography)*

Above: *Dancers twirl down Mission Street during the Cinco de Mayo parade in San Francisco's Mission District. (Photograph © Kerrick James)*

Right: *During Chinese New Year, celebrants parade through the streets of Chinatown with giant, colorful fabric dragons. (Photograph © Kerrick James)*

The lights of downtown San Francisco offer an enchanting view from this neighborhood hilltop. (Photograph © Frank S. Balthis)

Facing page: *The Columbus tower, built in 1905, stands in stark contrast to the ultra-modern Transamerica Building, built in 1971. (Photograph © Larry Ulrich/ Larry Ulrich Stock Photography)*

Above: *The majestic Plaster Palace, part of the Palace of Fine Arts, was designed by Bernard Maybeck for the Panama Pacific Exhibition in 1915. (Photograph © Dietrich Leis Stock Photography)*

Facing page: *Pigeon Point Lighthouse rises from the mist along Highway 1, near the town of Pescadero. The light, named for a ship that once ran aground here, first brightened the night sky in 1872. (Photograph © Willard Clay)*

Above: *South of Davenport, the fading sun warms the sandstone headlands. (Photograph © Larry Ulrich/ Larry Ulrich Stock Photography)*

Flowering ice plants adorn the sandstone arch at Natural Bridges State Beach near Point Santa Cruz. (Photograph © Willard Clay)

Left: *Breaking waves and high surf make the California coast a popular destination for surfboarders. (Photograph © Larry Ulrich/ Larry Ulrich Stock Photography)*

A surfer catches a wave near Santa Cruz, a town so dedicated to the sport that it opened a surfing museum. (Photograph © Frank S. Balthis)

The Beach Boardwalk Amusement Park is one of Santa Cruz's main attractions. Tourists come to Santa Cruz just to ride on the Giant Dipper, a wooden roller coaster built in the 1920s that is now an historic landmark. (Photograph © Larry Ulrich/ Larry Ulrich Stock Photography)

A colorful apartment community borders the waterfront in the beach town of Capitola. (Photograph © Gary Crabbe/Enlight-ened Images)

The giant boulder that rests in Morro Bay was once a point of navigation for early Spanish explorers. On shore, rolling sand dunes give way to beaches laden with clams. (Photograph © Dietrich Leis Stock Photography)

Facing page: *The surf swirls around the jagged rocks just below the Cypress Grove Trail at Point Lobos State Reserve. (Photograph © Mary Liz Austin)*

Left: *A drive along Highway 1 provides stunning views of the Monterey Coast. (Photograph © Londie G. Padelsky)*

Sea otters are a common sight in Monterey Bay. (Photograph © Mark Conlin/ Larry Ulrich Stock Photography)

Facing page: *Sticky monkey flowers bloom along the bluffs of Montana de Oro State Park. In the summertime, this 8,000-acre park is home to the monarch butterfly. (Photograph © J. C. Leacock)*

Above: *The Seven Gables Inn is one of many bed and breakfasts in the sleepy town of Pacific Grove on the Monterey coast. (Photograph © Larry Ulrich/Larry Ulrich Stock Photography)*

Above: *Although its exterior is simple and understated, Mission San Miguel's elaborately painted interior features an all-seeing eye. The mission was founded near San Luis Obispo in 1797. (Photograph © Carolyn Fox/Image West Photography)*

A statue of Junípero Serra, the Franciscan priest who founded several of the missions along El Camino Real, stands watch over Mission San Antonio, near Los Robles. (Photograph ©Larry Angier/Image West Photography)

On a hillside in Santa Clara County, horses and cattle graze on spring's new growth. (Photograph © Gary Crabbe/Enlightened Images)

California's Central Valley, with its fertile, sandy soil and extensive irrigation systems, provides an ideal climate for growing a wide variety of crops. (Photograph © Gary Crabbe/ Enlightened Images)

Peach trees thrive in an orchard near Maxwell in Colusa County. (Photograph © Gary Crabbe/Enlightened Images)

A blue oak stretches its giant limbs over the rolling, grassy Sierra Nevada foothills. (Photograph © Dennis Flaherty)

Facing page: *A serene path, scattered with fallen, yellow aspen leaves, invites hikers to explore this Sierra Nevada forest. (Photograph © Dennis Flaherty)*

Left: *In the depths of autumn, aspen leaves in varying shades of yellow and orange provide a thick, protective covering for the forest floor. (Photograph © Dennis Flaherty)*

Below: *Golden autumn leaves contrast sharply with the crisp blue of the Sierra Nevada sky. (Photograph © Dennis Flaherty)*

Left: *A road winds through the giant trees in Sequoia National Park. Sequioa and its sister park, Kings Canyon, contain thirty-four groves combined. (Photograph © Dietrich Leis Stock Photography)*

Top: *The weathered bristlecone pines of California's White Mountains are believed to be even older than the ancient sequoias. (Photograph © Chuck Place/Place Stock Photo)*

Bottom: *Balancing Rock rests precariously just beneath Moro Rock, at the edge of Giant Forest, Sequioa National Park. (Photograph © Chuck Place/Place Stock Photo)*

Facing page: *The grassy banks of the Owens River offer a stunning view of the Sierra Nevada range at daybreak. (Photograph © Dennis Flaherty)*

Left: *A camper enjoys the silence and calm of the Alabama Hills at night. (Photograph © Larry Prosor)*

At 14,496 feet, Mount Whitney catches the first light of day. The jagged peak is the highest point on the continental United States. (Photograph © Londie G. Padelsky)

Facing page: *Snow-covered Mount Whitney and Lone Pine Peak rise above the Alabama Hills. (Photograph © Dennis Flaherty)*

Above: *Shaman petroglyphs decorate the walls of Little Petroglyph Canyon in California's Coso Mountains. (Photography © Dennis Flaherty)*

Right: *Dry desert winds created the ever-shifting Mesquite Flats Sand Dunes, near Stove Pipe Wells in Death Valley. (Photograph © Terry Donnelly)*

Below: *Death Valley's Zabriskie Point is one of the most beautiful areas of the park. (Photograph © Londie G. Padelsky)*

Mineral deposits and volcanic ash paint the gravel at Artist's Palette in a rainbow of colors. (Photograph © Gary Alan Nelson)

Left: *Springtime showers the desert floor with blooming wildflowers. Desert sunflower grows in the valley over-looking Telescope Peak, the highest mountain in the Panamint Range. (Photograph © Larry Ulrich/ Larry Ulrich Stock Photography)*

Top: *A Specter Phacelia begins to bloom in Death Valley National Park. (Photograph © Dennis Flaherty)*

Bottom: *Droplets of dew settle on the leaves of a miniature lupine in the Sierra Nevada foothills. (Photograph © Dennis Flaherty)*

Above: *The bell towers of Mission Santa Barbara are bathed in the light of a full moon. The mission, founded in 1786, was the tenth mission built along El Camino Real in California. (Photograph © Chuck Place/Place Stock Photo)*

Facing page: *The Spanish built fortresses like the Presidio in Santa Barbara to protect the mission settlements along the coast. The fort and its chapel, shown here, are now part of El Presidio de Santa Barbara State Historic Park. (Photograph © Chuck Place/Place Stock Photo)*

Right: *Cowboy Ray Garcia ropes cattle in the Owens Valley. (Photograph © Londie G. Padelsky)*

Below: *Dust flies and the thunder clouds roll in during a cattle roundup in the Owens Valley. (Photograph © Londie G. Padelsky)*

Over thousands of years, wind and rain have shaped the towering spires and cliffs of Red Rock Canyon. (Photograph © Dennis Flaherty)

Facing page: *The palm trees, fountain, and ambient lighting lend a typically Californian air to Acapulco Restaurant in Santa Barbara. (Photograph © Chuck Place/Place Stock Photo)*

Above: *The setting sun warmly reflects off the Sierra Madre Mountains, providing the perfect backdrop to Santa Barbara's tranquil harbor. (Photograph © Chuck Place/Place Stock Photo)*

A couple takes an evening stroll through Palisades Park, a strip of lush greenery that stretches along the beach in Santa Monica. (Photograph © Gary Crabbe/Enlightened Images)

The Santa Monica Pier has been a popular summertime destination for area residents and tourists alike since 1908. (Photograph © Gary Crabbe/Enlightened Images)

Right: *Surfers catch waves and sunbathe at LA's Manhattan Beach. (Photograph © Gary Crabbe/Enlightened Images)*

Manhattan Beach, accessible via the coastal bike path, is a favorite destination for sport enthusiasts. (Photograph © Gary Crabbe/Enlightened Images)

Paths wind along the cliffs above Laguna Beach in Orange County, making it a great place to watch the sun go down. (Photograph © Gary Crabbe/Enlightened Images)

From aptly named Inspiration Point, visitors to beautiful Anacapa Island in Channel Islands National Park can watch the sun cast the first rays of light across the volcanic island chain. (Photograph © J. C. Leacock)

Left: *Channel Islands National Park provides a haven for wildlife, including dolphins, gray whales, sea lions, cormorants, and fox. (Photograph © J. C. Leacock)*

The rolling green hills of Santa Cruz Island are part of a Nature Conservancy preserve. (Photograph © J. C. Leacock)

Crystal Pier on San Diego's Pacific Beach is an ideal place to fish, watch surfers, or admire the sunset. (Photograph © Chuck Place/Place Stock Photo)

The walking paths of the Embarcadero along San Diego's waterfront link popular sights such as the Broadway Pier, the Maritime Museum, and Seaport Village. (Photograph © Chuck Place/Place Stock Photo)

The classic Victorian-style Hotel del Coronado has been a San Diego institution since it was built in 1888. Over the years, guests have included Franklin D. Roosevelt and Marilyn Monroe. (Photograph © Gary Crabbe/Enlightened Images)

San Diego's well-known Balboa Park was established in 1868 and is home to museums, botanical gardens, and the zoo. Many of the buildings that appear throughout the park, such as Casa del Prado, pictured here, were built in the Spanish style for the 1915 Panama-Pacific Exposition. (Photograph © Chuck Place/Place Stock Photo)

Left: *Colorful umbrellas shield diners from the intense California sun at Casa de Pico Restaurant in Old Town San Diego State Historic Park. Located north of downtown, Old Town was the original city center. (Photograph © Chuck Place/Place Stock Photo)*

Below: *Mexican dancers entertain at Old Town's Bazaar del Mundo, a Mexican-style plaza lined with shops and restaurants. (Photograph © Chuck Place/Place Stock Photo)*

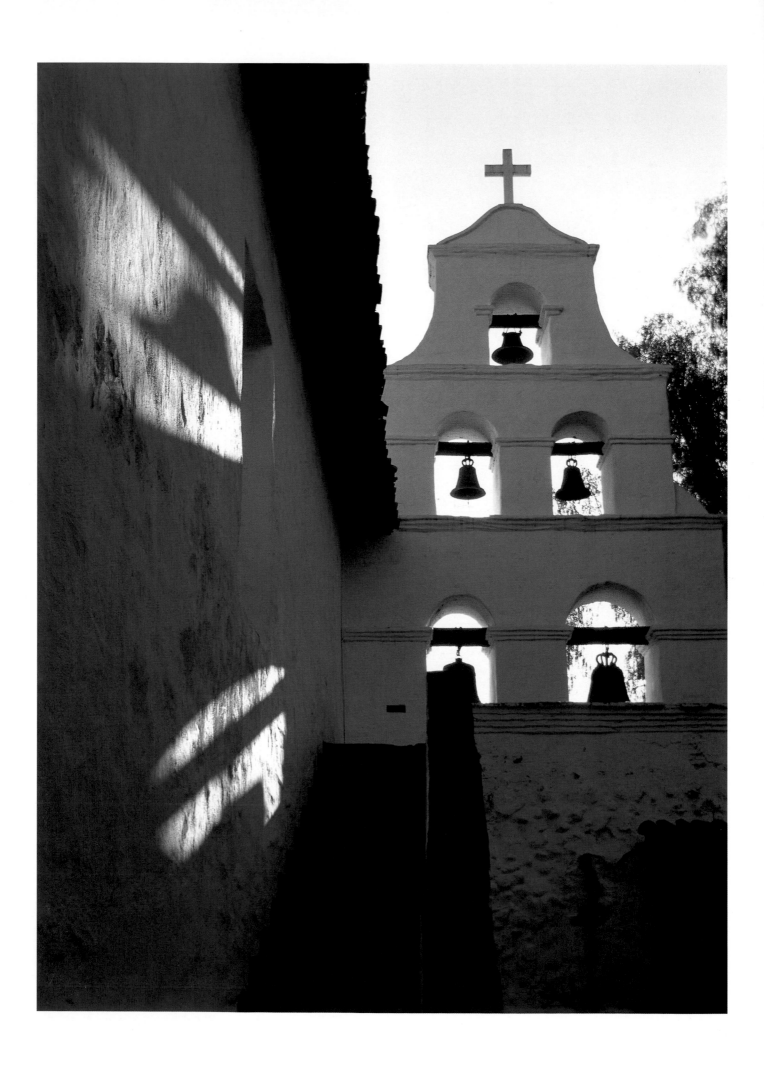

Facing page: *The bell tower of Mission San Diego de Alcalá casts a shadow on the courtyard wall. Established in its present location in 1774, the mission was California's first. (Photograph © Carolyn Fox/Image West Photography)*

Above: *From 1855 until 1891, Old Point Loma Lighthouse marked the entrance to San Diego Bay. (Photograph © Dietrich Leis Stock Photography)*

Waves crash onto the beach at Torrey Pines State Reserve, north of San Diego. The reserve's dry, sandy landscape provides the perfect environment for Torrey pines, trees that date from before the Ice Age. (Photograph © Londie G. Padelsky)

Hiking trails wind along the top of the eroded sandstone cliffs at Torrey Pines. (Photograph © Larry Ulrich/Larry Ulrich Stock Photography)

Facing page: *Bright yellow brittlebush and red chuparosa provide a blaze of color near Borrego Palm Canyon, Anza-Borrego Desert State Park. (Photograph © Terry Donnelly)*

Left: *The beavertail cactus blooms from March through June in the desert's dry, rocky hills. (Photograph © Terry Donnelly)*

The rising sun casts a splash of light across the Borrego Badlands and San Felipe Wash, Anza-Borrego Desert State Park. (Photograph © Terry Donnelly)

Right: *A Joshua tree erupts in light-green blooms, Joshua Tree National Park. The trees belong to the yucca family, and some may grow as tall as 30 feet. (Photograph © Willard Clay)*

Above: *Rock formations near the Jumbo Rocks area of Joshua Tree National Park took shape long ago when molten lava surfaced, cooled, and then shifted with the movement of the earth. (Photograph © J. C. Leacock)*

Facing page: *Joshua trees in the park's Hidden Valley area appear to reach for the moon. (Photograph © J. C. Leacock)*

A California juniper leans toward a rock formation, creating a natural arch in Joshua Tree National Park. (Photograph © Dennis Flaherty)